Headhunter

Published by Accent Press Ltd – 2014

ISBN 9781783754908

The Quick Reads project in Wales is an initiative coordinated by
the Welsh Books Council and supported by the Welsh Government.

Printed and bound by CPI Group (UK) Ltd, Croydon, CR0 4YY

Cover design by Midnight Designs

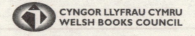

CYNGOR LLYFRAU CYMRU
WELSH BOOKS COUNCIL

Noddir gan
Lywodraeth Cymru
Sponsored by
Welsh Government

Headhunter

Jade Jones

ACCENT PRESS LTD

Quick Reads 2014

Congratulations on choosing a 2014 Quick Read.

The Quick Reads project, with bite-sized books, is designed to get readers back into the swing of reading, and reading for pleasure. So we hope you enjoy this book.

What's your opinion?

Your feedback can make this project better. Once you've read one of the Quick Reads series, visit www.readingwales.org.uk or Twitter #quickreads2014 to post your feedback.
- Why did you choose this book?
- What did you like about it?
- What do you think of the Quick Reads series?
- Which Quick Reads would you like to see in the future?

What next?

Once you've finished one Quick Read – have you got time for another?

Look out for other titles in the 2014 Quick Reads series.

Taekwondo: 'the way of the foot and the hand'. Korean Martial Art

Chapter One

All the money I ever spent was worth every penny when they put that medal around her neck

Martin Foulkes, Jade's granddad

My granddad, Martin Foulkes, is my inspiration. He is the one who set me on the path to Olympic gold. He could see that I was getting a bit cheeky and mischievous as a small child and he wanted me to learn to defend myself and keep me off the streets. He also wanted to make sure that I had a good start and learnt respect, so, when I was eight years old, he took me to the local taekwondo club in my home town of Flint, north Wales ... the rest, as they say, is history!

I was always a very active child and very single-minded. One of my dad's friends had a glass jar in his room that he filled up with spare change. I was fascinated by all of the coins. He could see I was drawn towards it and teased me by saying,

'If you can lift and hold the jar out straight in front of you for three minutes, you can have it!' He thought there wasn't much chance of an eight-year-old girl succeeding in this task, but I was very strong and held it out for the full three minutes. He couldn't believe it, but had to give me the money as he'd agreed. I am strong and very determined when I put my mind to something. Granddad and Nana took me to try lots of different sports when I was small. As they put it, I tried everything else and then came taekwondo. I had been to gymnastics but it wasn't for me. I'd tried badminton, swimming, athletics, Morris dancing and they were all right for a couple of weeks but my heart wasn't in them and I didn't enjoy them enough to keep going. All that changed when I arrived at the Flint Taekwondo Club.

The coach at the club was Martin Williams. I looked around the room at what was going on and how he was working with other youngsters and knew immediately this was for me! I fell in love with all the flashy kicks and spins and couldn't take my eyes off what was happening. I looked at my granddad and he smiled, and he knew then that he had done exactly the right thing. This was the sport for me! It was really cool. Everywhere I looked there was action and I wanted to be part of it! I watched as they moved up and down the hall. All around me was a wall of noise. People were shouting at each other and having a great time. Flint Taekwondo Club was the place to be! I could see children of all ages and they all seemed to know what to do. Granddad asked me, 'Do you like it? Do you want to start?' He didn't need to ask twice – I was desperate to get going! I couldn't wait to try it out for myself.

The second time he took me, the very next week, my nana came too. She could see how excited I was and was intrigued to find out what was working its magic on me. I proudly entered the hall, dressed in my tracksuit bottoms and a T-shirt. I learnt a few basic moves and kicks and blocks and grinned with pride at her. Up and down the room we went, practising punches and kicks and, with every step, I enjoyed it more and more. Everything clicked into place. I loved it!

The coach knew quickly, too, that this was for me. He took my grandparents aside and said, 'She's a natural!' Granddad said that he always knew I had real potential and I was thrilled but very shy about showing just how much this meant to me. I wanted very much to do well, but I didn't tell anyone in school how good it had been. I didn't know what people would think of me doing this sport, and I wanted to keep it for myself.

I worked hard, practised, and I got better and better. I went to buy my first dobok (loose taekwondo clothes) from Martin's club and I wore it with pride. I hung it up in my bedroom and looked at it constantly. Granddad told me later that he waited some time before taking me to get my dobok because he wanted to make sure that I would stick with this sport before he spent a lot of money. He didn't want me changing my mind. However, my family could see how much it already meant to me and they took me wherever I needed to go. I went to classes four evenings a week and my grandparents drove me there each time. I began entering competitions straight away and started to win. I tried my hardest because I wanted to make my family proud of me. I loved the feeling of winning and I wanted to feel like that again and again. I wanted to be the best I could be.

I was only a yellow belt when I entered my first competition in Chester, and I had only been training for about three months so I was nervous but Granddad and Nana just said, 'Do

4

your best.' I wanted them to be proud of me and, with my chin up and my heart beating fast, I got started. I won bronze in sparring (fighting with an opponent) and couldn't put my medal down. There was no stopping me now. I'll never forget how excited I felt. I couldn't wait to get home and tell my mum and dad and all the family about it. It was official – I was hooked on this Korean martial art.

Chapter Two

She is the superstar in our sport. She does a great deal to promote our sport in the community without fuss.
David Baker, head coach of Matrix Taekwondo and the Welsh Commonwealth Taekwondo team coach

As a child I competed regularly all over Wales, England and Scotland. I gained over one hundred trophies from the Tae Kwon-do Association of Great Britain and became English, Welsh and Scottish champion. My family were always there for me. They would drive me to and from wherever I needed to go and supported me every inch of the way. They built up my confidence so that I started to believe that I could do well. I enjoyed the training sessions too, but I was still very quiet in situations I didn't know and didn't have a lot of self-confidence. I was friendly with a girl called Natalie Simpson and we were serious in training but enjoyed a joke and a giggle out of class together. Every year at the Christmas party she had the confidence to get up and dance but I was far too shy, no matter how much I wanted to. However, in taekwondo, people began to notice that there were very few events where I didn't win medals. Even other instructors praised me, telling me I had promise, and that built my confidence. The highlight was becoming double British Champion, black stripe belt, at the age of eleven, in patterns (an ordered sequence of moves) and in sparring.

Granddad and Nana were so proud of me, and having them there to share my success meant everything. My mum and my dad were often working but they still put such a lot into my success. I had to go to Bristol to take my black belt grading and I was very nervous indeed, especially as they didn't give me my result at the time, which made me worry even more. All of us in the club were pleased for each other's successes. We trained together and were mates and wanted the best for each other. We learnt new patterns together and knew all the work that had gone into our grading. I was delighted to get my black belt and we all celebrated our results. I couldn't believe it!

As I got better, there were additional classes in Wrexham and Chester and even as far away as Cardiff, where Sunday sessions were held above a bed shop in Roath. It meant going up and down the length of Wales in one day, as I had to be back for school on Monday, though school never made a fuss about this. Granddad and I used to squabble in the car about any little thing – what was good on the radio, where we would stop for food, how fast we were travelling. Nana had to be referee when we both turned to her and asked her to support us. She'd say, 'Keep me out of it!' It was all good fun. I was really excited at doing these extra teaching sessions. Granddad and Nana would wake me up very early in the morning and Granddad would sort my breakfast, then I'd go in and train and then get into the car, where I'd put my coat and a pillow, plump up the pillow and sleep most of the journey. The Sunday sessions were led by Gianni Peros, who was an amazing coach and a perfectionist. Whenever he took a session you could hear a pin drop. We had total respect for him. He never needed to lose his temper as we all concentrated on whatever he gave us to do. He would demonstrate moves in front of us and I always remember that he looked crisp in his dobok, with never a crease in it. I used to wonder how he could get out of the car, unbuckle his seat belt but never look crumpled like the rest of us! He would pull people out of training who were good and get them to come to the front and show the rest of the group. This was ultimate praise and if I was called to the front, I would be desperate to tell my mum and dad. All these extra sessions really helped me. Some people thought I was crazy going up and down to Cardiff on a Sunday, on top of all the other sessions in the week. My friends, too, would ask why I couldn't come out with them on a Sunday. But I could see the difference the extra training was making.

My parents were amazed at my success and, like my grandparents, extremely proud of me. My mum is my biggest fan but gets so nervous that she finds it hard to watch me fight. She doesn't want anyone to hurt me! She is concerned for me weeks before any fight. Whatever happens, whether I win or lose, she thinks I'm the best and that's great! I love taking her to special events as she is so pleased for me that it is a joy for me to be able to give her a treat. My dad and I built a gym in the spare bedroom so I could use it to train. Dad could see that I would try anything to improve myself – he even put up a punch-bag! But my dad is also too nervous to watch me fight. He hates thinking that someone could hurt me and has to close his eyes when I'm fighting. He's also scared of flying, so hasn't been able to come to lots of my competitions. Thank goodness the 2012 Olympics were in London!

My brother, Luke, is amazing. He was never jealous of all the attention I got. And he was always really pleased for me when I won and relaxed about people talking about what I had done. Like all younger brothers, he used to play-fight with me and I insisted that he was needed for my practice! When he was very young, I used to dress him up in a taekwondo suit and try to teach him. I would roll the sleeves and trousers up and get him to copy me ... I even have pictures of this! I don't know how he put up with me. He enjoys some rewards now, though. He says that it's great being my brother, as girls ask him if he is related to me. It's a great way to start chatting them up. Also, in school, if he had been put into the corridor for being naughty and a teacher arrived to question him, he is able to turn the conversation to news of me. 'How's Jade doing, Luke?' they'd ask and his behaviour was forgotten. He would phone to tell me, saying, 'Phew, got out of trouble today because …' Suddenly, he saw the benefit! I am lucky that my family are always there for me.

My school, Flint High School, was very proud of my success. I was always good at sport; PE and cookery were my favourite lessons. I can remember really impressing myself by making an apple crumble in Miss Lynskey's lessons. I carried it home waiting for my family to tell me how great it was, but they were a bit scared to eat it! Looking back, probably apple crumble was my only big success in the kitchen. In PE though, I was a proper success, but not the only one in the school. Three pupils represented Wales, one at women's football, one at swimming and me. I enjoyed netball, ran in the cross-country team for Flintshire, and played rounders and rugby. I was keen to be a part of any team I could get into. My games teacher, Mrs Teasdale Jones, always worked hard to build my confidence. She was understanding when I had to rush off to competitions and helped me believe in myself. Her advice was simple and clear: 'Keep training hard and you'll go far.' While some teachers might not have been too happy to let me go off to competitions, Mrs Teasdale Jones could see how much it meant to me and offered only encouragement. Mind you, at one time she did try to get me to join the netball team and to cut back on my taekwondo training! We laugh about this now! Taekwondo was my dream and I wanted everyone to see what it meant to me. Mrs McClean, my headmistress, was always equally supportive. She could see this was my passion and she knew how much I was giving up to progress. Even though I left school at sixteen, I still sat my GCSE examinations – in a training camp in Manchester. It wasn't like being in school sitting your exams with your mates around you but we had no choice. I sat my exams surrounded by older people, people I didn't know, but I was in training for the Junior European Championships in Sweden and this was the only way to do it.

My coach in this early period was very special. I have a great deal to thank Martin Williams for. Joining his classes inspired me to believe that I could do well in this sport. He was extremely technical with amazing kicks. He gave me a solid base to work from. He would give me extra tasks to do in classes to improve my leg strength and he took time and gave my friends and me extra tuition. In school, and in my chosen sport, I began to realise the importance of teachers and coaches. The really good ones give up so much of themselves, so that others can succeed. They were a very important part of my road towards gold.

Chapter Three

I can see how hard she works and how much she wants it ... Every target you put in front of her she meets.

Brian Green, coach of Manchester Aces

My next goal was to work towards the European Championships in Cork, Ireland, where I became European Champion at sparring. I represented TAGB Wales (Tae Kwon-do Association of Great Britain) at adult level at the age of fifteen. I was really excited to be asked to step into the team at the last moment. Gianni Peros and Joe Schembri were in charge of the Wales team and I knew how important this competition was to them. It was a big step up for me, and my nana was scared for me and didn't want me to do it. Granddad did though, and his encouragement convinced me. 'I think you're good enough,' was all he said. He didn't need to say more – I knew that was praise enough from him. I was on a huge high after winning the junior competition, so to be asked join the adult team was the best!

The crowd screamed as I stepped up ready to compete. There was a large group from south Wales and the atmosphere in the hall was bouncing. The score was already one each and mine was to be the deciding fight. The crowd went quiet, the names were familiar ... England versus Wales. No pressure, then! I took a deep breath and got ready to fight.

When I won, the crowd let out a mighty roar and the scene became absolutely crazy. People were hugging each other and jumping up and down and screaming. I was looking out for my family. Then I saw Nana, screeching and leaping about in a frenzy. I'd done well! I had helped Wales to win the team competition. The team were thrilled and Jess Howells from the team came up to me, jumping with joy and cried, 'You did it!' The after-party was a great celebration – Scottish, Irish, English and Welsh all celebrating together. It was good to see how everyone celebrated other teams' achievements. One fan wasn't too happy, though, as he came up to me at the end and muttered, 'I've got an awful sore throat shouting for you, Jade!'

Granddad kept looking out for new and

better training and learning opportunities for me as he could see I was desperate to be the best I could possibly be. He found a class at the Morgan Llwyd Sports Centre in Wrexham with David Baker, head coach of Matrix Taekwondo. It was a twenty-mile journey from Flint to Wrexham, but we did it because we knew this was the way to learn from some of the best. Paul Green came there to do a taekwondo seminar. He was a ten-times British Champion, numerous-times European Champion, World Silver medallist and Olympic quarter-finalist. I loved watching him perform the full-contact version of the sport where you could hit as hard as you liked, and I knew that was what I wanted to do. I loved the tactical element. He was so fast and strong and his kicks were unbelievable. Just looking at him made me want to be that good. He seemed superhuman when he kicked, faster than I had ever seen anyone kick before. I went up to get his autograph, completely in awe of him. His father, Brian Green, asked me what club I was from and I was thrilled that he had taken the trouble to talk to me. In our sport, recognition from another coach is a great compliment. I can remember being so excited by what Paul could do and knowing that his full-contact type of taekwondo was the way I wanted to go. I needed to move away from semi-contact, which was what I'd been doing up till then. My Olympic dream was building.

In changing from the Tae Kwon-do Association to the WTF (World Taekwondo Federation), I could follow my dream – to make the Olympic Games. I stayed with David's group for a while, but to his credit, he talked to us and said, 'We only have one class a week. She needs more training than we can offer at the moment.' I have great respect for him as he could have kept me with him, but he was an honourable man and wanted the best for me. He could see that changing to the contact sport would really suit me. He told us to go to the Manchester Aces Taekwondo Club in Manchester run by Brian Green, Paul's father, who David had worked closely with. David's daughter Danielle had been taught by Brian in his club and she had been British champion three times and twice Commonwealth medallist. Brian assessed me and at the end told my granddad, 'She's a rough diamond. We can do something with her. We can polish her up.' I am so grateful he saw something in me. The change to the World

Taekwondo Federation and training in Manchester meant that I was on my way – but yet more driving for Granddad and Nana! I didn't lose contact with David totally, though, as he put me in for regional competitions while I was starting training with Brian Green and he coached me for a competition in Holland. David also worked with Sport Wales and British Taekwondo to create the pathway that eventually allowed me to join the GB Taekwondo Academy. We kept good ties with each other. He has said that it is because of my success that there are more taekwondo clubs in north Wales. He calls it 'Jade's legacy'. He is extremely pleased that all the extra classes that opened up because of me are still full. I am proud to be what he calls 'the female role model' if it means more girls take part in this great sport.

Changing from the Tae Kwon-do Association of Great Britain to the World Taekwondo Federation was daunting from the onset. It is a totally different style of fighting and requires a different level of fitness. I found it tough moving from semi-contact to full contact. There was no protective footwear in WTF as there was in TAGB. Now I had to kick with my bare feet against a hard chest pad. I had to toughen up quickly. If you switch off for one second you can be knocked out. I came home a bit battered and bruised occasionally. Sometimes I felt completely shattered but I kept it to myself. I kept getting beaten in training but it made me train harder. I wondered whether I had done the right thing. I lost the first few competitions and it was hard going from being the top fighter in TAGB to bottom in the WTF. I was a very small fish in a very big pond, a nobody. It was really difficult, thinking one minute you're good, and then realising quite how much you have yet to learn! In one fight I was winning but ended up losing by one point. I could have won but I didn't know the new rules correctly. I didn't make that mistake again. I took the competitions one by one and refused to feel defeated. I had to learn. I knew I had to up my game. I lost a lot of smaller competitions and it would have been easy to give up, but I didn't. Looking back, I can see how important losing really is. I had to learn to lose to really appreciate winning. I'm glad that I had Brian to guide me. He made sure that each tournament was a little harder and each win built my confidence. He wanted to make sure that I proved my worth at each stage. I won in the National Championships in Manchester and Brian's message was an important one: 'It's easy to be National Champion. We'll start fighting abroad and see how you get on there.'

The first competition abroad was the Dutch Open where I lost to a German girl. I was embarrassed and it didn't feel nice losing. I wasn't used to feeling like this. At that time, I didn't really talk to any of the competitors from other countries, as I was so in awe of them. They all looked confident and I felt too shy. But it was interesting to see all of the different teams from so many countries and look at the different ways they prepared. The French always looked smart and as if they meant business!

My next major competition was at the French Open, which was a very important competition. I remember the final well as I'd had six fights already, which was a lot in a competition, and then had to face the Russian fighter. She was tall and very strong and I felt tired out. I only had ten to fifteen minutes' rest before they called on me to fight the final. Brian was there supporting and encouraging me. He made sure I had the proper rest time and that I was ready. As I went to go to fight, he said, 'Come on Jade, just one more!' It was a close fight but the result made the crowd roar and the cheers started. I had done it! I stood on the podium with a smile from ear to ear. I held the massive trophy aloft and grinned with pleasure, unable to take it all in. Everyone was laughing at me as they watched me smiling non-stop! Finally, it had all clicked into place. I had made the right decision.

Brian Green was amazed that I'd won, beating competitors from all over the world. He said that people trained all their lives and never got the chance to win at such a major competition. People really did start to take notice now: a girl who'd come out of nowhere and gained such a great achievement. My family was clear that it was all down to Brian and Paul and the coaching I was getting. Much later, Brian told me that I had surpassed every goal he had set me and that was praise indeed from him. I didn't know that he had already marked me out as Academy potential but he was teaching me to earn my place and not expect instant rewards and fame.

Following on from the French Open victory, I was picked to go to the Junior World

Championships in Mexico to represent Great Britain for the first time, the junior qualifications for the Youth Olympics. The Junior World Championships were held one week after the Youth Olympics qualification tournament, also in Mexico. We had to raise £1500 for the flights and hotels, and that was a lot of money for my family to find. It was really tough but the community of Flint pulled together to help us. There were raffles and events and all the people of Flint chipped in. It was brilliant to know that everyone was there for me. There was even a special big day to raise money when all the local pubs held events. They did all of this without knowing whether I might even be in the running for a medal.

But I got a bronze in the qualifications tournament, and that was all that was needed to qualify. I then withdrew to save myself for the Junior World Championships. I fought against the Korean girl who was the best in the sport, and won the silver medal. At the time I was training for four hours a week and competing against someone who was training full time, so I was thrilled with this. Suddenly, in the fight, I started to believe in myself. I started to gain confidence and I said to myself,

'You can do this!' I realised just how far I had come and that nothing was going to pull me down. My coach for this was Sarah Stevenson, the first British Taekwondo World Champion and the bronze medallist at the Beijing Olympic Games in 2008. Sarah did a fantastic job getting me a World silver medal in her first coaching role and I couldn't thank her enough. 2010 was a great year for me – I was awarded Jaguar Rising Star of the Future, BBC Wales Junior Sportsperson of the Year and British Olympic Association Taekwondo Athlete of the Year. Things were beginning to come together.

My dream now was to train at the GB Taekwondo Academy in Manchester, with Paul Green as my coach. I asked every week, 'Can I go into the Academy now?', driving everyone mad. Brian, ever wise, told me, 'You don't want to go in there too early. Take your time.' I was over-eager and Brian held me back until he was sure, because I had a lot of learning to do. I would come away from fights bruised and pounded, with a few tears, but it only made me more determined to succeed. I put my total faith in Brian. He would always say to me, 'Fight well. I don't care if you get beaten but fight well.'

Gary Hall, the Performance Director of GB

Taekwondo, finally made the decision that I was ready to go to the Academy and that all of Brian's work had paid off. He met Brian and my grandparents in Manchester to discuss the arrangements. I would move to the Academy at the age of seventeen, and there were lots of questions to answer as to who I would stay with and who would look after me, as I was still young. I had just started at Deeside College doing a BTEC qualification in sport, but this would have to change. I would pull out of college and go to Manchester full-time to start my new life. I was so lucky that my mum and dad and all my family supported me. I was ecstatic and even more so because they told me that the reason the decision was made to let me go to the Academy was that I was a hope for 2012, the London Olympic Games. It was a slim chance but I believed I could do it.

Chapter Four

She has an immense talent at a very young age. She is mature in her approach to a competitive career and is always willing to listen and learn. She is a true champion.

Dame Kelly Holmes, double Olympic gold medallist 800 and 1500 metres

My new flat was shared with Bianca Walkden, who was also in the Academy. We clicked immediately and became close mates. She was great to live with as she was lively and talkative and she looked after me like a sister. I was quiet and shy but she kept me going. She was a year older than me and already knew so much more than me about looking after herself. She did all the cooking and cleaning as I had never done any of these things for myself, and I didn't know where to start, other than making apple crumble! She cooked chicken and pasta and laughed that it was a good job she did the cooking, as otherwise I would just be eating cereal out of the box! I was hopeless at housework too, and had to rely on her to help me out. I didn't know how to use the washing machine. I had to learn from her how to wash my training kit and hang it properly to dry. At home, I'd been very lucky as my mum had done everything for me, but now I had to learn to fend for myself. I'd always had my meals cooked for me. Once, I was making toast in the flat and I couldn't get the toast out of the toaster, so I tried sticking my fingers into the metal slot on the top! No one could believe it. Bianca and I both laugh at just how much she had to teach me. She brought me out of myself and encouraged me to join her in the gym rather than quietly stretch on my own. It was good for us both, as up until then she had been the only girl training and she found it great to have company. We would come back from training, have a quick shower, eat and then chill out watching TV, checking our laptops and phones and eating Haribos together. Every so often, Bianca would come up with something different from our usual after-training routine. She would suggest going to a café for dinner, or having a picnic or a kick about with a football outside.

I was on a six-month trial at the Academy,

hungry to do well and prove myself and, most importantly, make my trial permanent. I went to Singapore to compete at the Youth Olympics. I arrived late at the athletes' village, which wasn't great as everyone else had come together and now knew one another. At the time, I thought Paul, my coach, was mean not letting me join the others going to the games room, and not letting me go to the opening ceremony. He told me to knuckle down to training and said, 'If you don't get gold, all this will mean nothing.' He was so right. Who would remember the time spent messing about? I was so lucky to have Paul and realised he had my best interests at heart in every decision he made. He taught me the importance of drive and determination. I didn't let up because he believed in me and I wanted to prove I deserved his trust.

I had four fights in Singapore, against fighters from Ivory Coast, Mexico, Sweden and Vietnam. I felt good and thought that I could do this. It was the first Youth Olympics and the first chance of a gold medal for Great Britain. I just kept thinking to myself, this will show them that I am capable of performing on the big stage. They will know I'm ready for London

2012. My mum said that every time I came out I looked like a ghost because I was so nervous. But I'm always like that. I always feel nervous leading up to the competition, sometimes getting really emotional the night before. It's because I want to win so much. I put everything into my fight and the build-up is crucial to me. However, as soon as my foot steps on the mat, it's all gone and I am ready! I never worry about getting hurt. For me, it's about not wanting to lose. I won't let myself think that I can lose. The days leading up to a fight are the worst for me and the waiting is agony. Once everything starts, I am in the zone and ready.

The best was to happen in Singapore. I won the gold medal, beating the Vietnamese competitor in the final. All of my family were there. I can remember looking up to see them – and most definitely hearing them! It was fantastic for me, as I hadn't seen my family for seven weeks while I had been in training camps in China and Korea. The team from BBC's *Blue Peter* was out there to film with Helen Skelton for a programme on the Youth Olympics. I did an interview with Helen after each fight and after the first day I told her that I would have to raise my game or I'd be going home. On the day of the fight, Helen was with my family all day finding out their thoughts on my journey to the competition. She was a big star in Singapore and soon everyone was crowded around her wanting photos and autographs. She asked them all to do her a favour in return. She asked that when I came out that they all scream for me. They were happy to do that for her and the noise was unbelievable. I kept looking around wondering why all these people I had never met before were screaming my name! Paul looked up in shock, unsure what was going on as hundreds of people were shouting 'Jade!' I had the best support ever! When I returned to the village that night there was even a poster on my door saying 'congratulations'. I don't know to this day who it was from!

People often ask me if I have any superstitions before a match. Do I have to do things in a particular way, or eat the same thing? For me, it's down to my granddad's boots ... It started at my first competition. He wore a pair of trainers and I got it into my head that they were lucky for me and that he always had to wear them. Every time I had a big competition, I insisted that he wore them. One time, he went on holiday and couldn't be there, so I begged my mum to wear them instead. I told her that they were essential. She refused to put them on, but brought them with her! Sadly, the shoes fell to bits over time, but I always remember them. At London 2012, I had a pink London 2012 band that I wore the whole time. I wore it every single day in the lead-up to the start of the fights but as the competition started properly, and just as I was about to go on, they made me take it off. Before I could worry about it, Paul pulled it over his wrist saying, 'Don't worry, I'll wear it for you.' He could see how much it meant to me and stepped in just in time to save the day.

Before the Youth Olympics, I had won a bursary from the Jaguar Academy and had had guidance from their elite athletes. I won the Jaguar Academy of Sport Special Recognition award and Star of the Future award in the first Jaguar Academy of Sport awards in 2010. It was a spectacular evening held at Lord's Cricket Ground in London. All the great athletes were there and my mum and I looked around the room spotting faces and nudging each other in excitement. I remember sitting next to Dame Kelly Holmes, my hero, and being amazed to be in a room with top athletes that I could only dream about ever being like. The building itself was very grand and every table was packed with the top names in sport. On each table were miniature cricket bats to collect autographs on, but I was far too shy to ask and had to get Darren, my stepdad, to go around and ask for me. I was presented with a massive trophy in a huge box and started to worry about how we would get it back to the hotel on the London Underground. We had no idea of the underground and platforms, and ended up leaving Darren with the trophy on the station as we leapt onto the train and the doors shut behind us! Darren pretended he was stuck and we began to panic – only to learn he had found a quicker train and got back to the hotel before us!

The Jaguar Academy really helped focus me on my future. It was set up to inspire the next generation of British sporting heroes by giving them the opportunity to work with and learn from the best British sportsmen and women. My mentor was my hero, Dame Kelly Holmes. Kelly was very down to earth and yet was an Olympic double gold medallist. I wanted to be like her. She believed in me before I won anything. The mentoring days were excellent as I could get advice and guidance from people who had achieved all I wanted to achieve. She spoke about her passion to help young people fulfil their potential and just listening to her was inspirational. She gave us positive messages and the confidence to believe in our future. I learnt a lot from her about how she dealt with the problems of injury. I tried to take in everything she said to us. She taught me that you should never give up. She was very clear that how we conducted ourselves as athletes was important and we all admired her professionalism. I only hoped that if I was ever really successful, I would handle it like her. I had no idea that I would one day be part of Jaguar's ambassador team.

I also met Jamie Baulch, one of the most decorated British athletes. He told me that he thought I had real potential and that was praise indeed. A year later, in a meeting at the Lowry Hotel in Manchester, he questioned me about how I saw my future. He asked me what I thought I could achieve at London 2012. He wrote down all my hopes and ambitions and raised his eyebrows when I announced my main ambition: 'To win gold at London 2012'.

Afterwards he told me that he was impressed by the calm and firm way that I repeated, 'I'm going to win.' He asked me if that was what I genuinely thought and I told him I was in no doubt. He said that it seemed almost like a formality to me and he admired my honest response. Then he agreed to become my sports agent. He told me that he wanted to look after athletes who worked hard and who had an inner belief and strength, and he saw that in me.

At this time, I was also nominated for the BBC Wales 'Junior Sportswoman of the Year' but I didn't think I had any chance at all. My travel to the event was chaotic. I was supposed to meet my granddad and nana in Flint but got on the wrong train and noticed I was heading to Blackpool! However, I didn't panic as I thought I'd just been invited to go to see the ceremony. At that stage I had no idea I was nominated for an award. I phoned Gary Hall to tell him my mistake and say that I was on my way back. He told me to stay in Manchester and arranged for me to be picked up by someone from the taekwondo team and taken to the ceremony, which was at the Celtic Manor, near Cardiff. I had twenty minutes to get in the shower and get myself ready! I was then told that I had been put up for an award, but I still had no idea what exactly was happening. It was a huge rush and I got myself ready in the car on the way down. The weather was dreadful with thick fog. At the ceremony I still had no idea what was happening when my name was called out. I was shocked to be told to go up on stage and couldn't believe that I had won against other great Welsh athletes. I was amazed that people even knew my name.

I was also named British Olympic Association Taekwondo Athlete of the Year. I had only been in the Academy for eight months, so to win this award was unbelievable. I was up against people I looked up to, like Sarah Stevenson, Bianca Walkden, Aaron Cook and others. It was a complete shock to see how delighted for me everyone was and how much they cared. Luckily, my friends had already thought that I might win and had taken time to make sure that I looked nice for the night. I'd kept telling them that I couldn't possibly win. Their faith in me meant the world to me.

Chapter Five

She's the best in the world at delivering under pressure when she needs to. She has drive and determination and never lets up.

Paul Green, coach GB Taekwondo

In 2011, I moved up to the senior level and just missed success in my first few competitions, only getting as far as the quarter finals. However, at the American Open in Texas, I won the bronze medal in my weight, the under 57 kg category. I was so disappointed with my result that I pestered my coach to let me fight the next day in the under 62 kg category, the higher weight. I was only 54 kg at the time, so I had to eat big meals and drink lots of water to get into the level. There was still a huge weight difference, but I was determined to try, and went up against the American girl, Paige McPherson, who was older and stronger than me. She was on her home turf and so the crowd was with her. It went to golden point – the first to score wins – and I won! I was seventeen years old and up against a very good fighter, but I had managed to win!

The trip wasn't all about competitions, though. We had to train for the fight in the hotel on a very dusty carpet, and we had to wear facemasks like doctors in an operating theatre to stop us coughing and spluttering from the dust. The photos we took were hilarious.

It really is true that everything is big in Texas. There were huge food portions but I wasn't complaining as I was well under my weight and could enjoy what was on offer. I felt really sorry for my teammates, though, who had to lose kilos and so watch everything they ate! We really enjoyed being in Texas, especially when we were in the hotel lift one day with a group of men who stared at us and said, 'Y'all ninjas?' when they found out we were the taekwondo team. We struck all the poses pretending we were ninjas and giggled our way out of the lift.

I also managed to win against Jonathan Ross on his TV show, much to the amusement of my friends. I was one of three Olympic hopefuls guesting on the show. Fran Halsall, the swimmer, heptathlete Louise Hazel and I were invited along to talk about our sporting past and dreams for 2012. I was wary of Jonathan, as people said he tended to poke fun at guests but he was really lovely and genuinely interested in what we were doing. We had a great time, as John Bishop and Brian Cox were also on the show and kept us laughing until the finale. I had to demonstrate my moves while the three men, suited up in protective gear, tried to fend me off. Jonathan was terrified as I moved towards him in full flight but the audience loved it! I tweeted afterwards, 'Had an amazing time filming for the Jonathan Ross show, but kicked John Bishop's elbow – hahaha.' I really enjoyed myself but I'm not so sure about Jonathan. What people didn't know was that before the show I had to practise with three members of the TV crew and one girl went down on the floor after I kicked her. Everyone laughed, thinking she was joking, but then quickly realised she was winded and had to be helped.

Soon afterwards, I was off to the German Open where I won the silver medal after losing out to a Croatian opponent. All of these competitions were building to qualify me to go to the World Championships in Korea in May

2011. I was still very young, and just after Korea the decision would be made by Gary Hall as to which weight had been chosen for London 2012. Looking back now, I can see how hard it must have been for him to choose who would go when three of us, Sarah, Bianca and I, were all involved. Bianca and I were sharing a room and it was hard for us knowing only one of us could go to the Olympic Games. Sarah would go anyway as she was clear favourite, which left only the one place between us. I went out and did everything I could to try to guarantee my spot for the Games. Luckily, in Korea I did very well, winning silver and missing gold by just one point against China and the current World Champion.

I had to keep proving myself to have a chance to compete at London 2012. But Gary Hall finally made my dream come true by selecting my weight. He wished me luck, told me to train hard and not to leave a stone unturned. I cried my eyes out and had to be in a room by myself to go over the decision in my mind. I wasn't allowed to tell anyone of the selection but my mum was creeping around outside the room trying to listen, and I think my response probably gave it away.

Gary Hall had put a great deal of faith in me as I was so young, and under 57 kg is a very competitive weight. I was very sorry for Bianca as she had been doing so well too, and despite being injured before the World Championships, had bravely come back determined to try. After the public announcement, she was heartbroken, as I would have been. I knew how I would have felt if the decision had been the other way. On the day, I was in the Academy sitting on my bed in the flat, embarrassed to go and see Bianca. I thought that I would be the last person she would want to see. It was very hard for both of us to be so close, to be living together, and to both want the same thing. We had been through so much together and knew how much we both wanted to go to London. But she came to congratulate me, told me how well I had done and wished me luck. I only hope that I would have been as gracious and generous in her position. She is a good friend and a great competitor, and I have no doubt she will be great in the future. Bring on Rio!

My boyfriend, Jordan Gayle, was also at the Academy. We are both very competitive and understand the stress and tension of competitions. He, too, had been injured before the London 2012 selection and was out of action for fifteen months with a career-threatening knee injury. I understood how he felt as we are both full contact martial arts athletes and are very aware of injury risks. Even though he was disappointed not to be going to London himself, he was thrilled for me and phoned to tell me, 'I believe in you. I'll be there to support you.' That meant the world to me. He, like Bianca, put me before his own feelings.

As soon as the announcement was made, Flint, my hometown, went crazy! There were 'Good Luck Jade' posters in what seemed like every house. There were pictures in shop windows and messages everywhere. People came up to me in the street to tell me how proud they were. There was a surprise party to celebrate the news and I begged my mum to invite only a few people. I walked into a party of hundreds! There were cameras flashing and people cheering and gifts to show how proud they all were of their local girl. I couldn't believe how many cards and gifts I was given. Flint High School had sent a school towel and mug and flowers, and it really did start to hit me how many people cared. People found time to send their very special things for me. There were numerous lucky angels and charms. My mum collected the coins with the taekwondo emblem that were quite hard to find. She believed that if she could find five coins it was a sign that I would win. She wanted to do anything to help me!

Then it was off to the team-holding camp in Loughborough and back to earth. It was strange for me as I was used to being with the full team, but now it was just the Olympic team of Sarah Stevenson, Martin Stamper, Lutalo Muhammad and me. Each of us had a training partner and mine was Paul, my coach. I went to collect my GB kit and I couldn't stop staring at the cases full of clothes and my Team GB holdall. Suddenly it was real. I was so proud and couldn't wait to wear the clothes. I tried them all on straight away, desperate to try everything, like a child in a sweet shop. I looked around at all the really famous athletes picking up their kit at the same time. It really came home to me that I was in their team too!

I was given a room by myself, which I was happy about. I like to be quiet and stay focused. I am shy and having space helps me to settle. I had time to think about just how far I had come and how much everyone had pulled together to help me get here. My family came to visit me at Loughborough, to keep me chilled out, they said. I showed them around the campus and we all went out to eat. They were surprised at how calm and relaxed I was as they expected a very different Jade at this point. But my family and Jordan had done everything for me. My mum and dad, my brothers, my stepdad Darren, my grandparents – they had all taken care of me to help me towards my ultimate goal. All my coaches had taken time and trouble to give their expertise. Brian's advice, as always, was important to me and he wanted me to realise just how big the Olympic Games were and that I would never face anything else like them. He talked about being privileged to qualify and I was grateful for his advice as ever.

Paul is an amazing coach and gave me the best preparation ever. I have absolute trust and belief in him. He went way beyond the call of duty to ensure that I was prepared for whatever the Olympics could bring. There were sixteen people I could have fought and each day he turned up for training as an opponent from a different country. We would go over and over their tactics and I knew all of my opponents inside out because of the work that we put in.

Every country and every opponent has a different style, and Paul would watch videos over and over again to get each style off by heart. He'd then fight me in their style so that I knew what I could expect. He would say, 'Right, I'll be China today', and he is so good that he could produce the exact style for me. The idea was to have no surprises when I fought. Lots of the other fighters would laugh when he was a female opponent and suggested getting him wigs!

Before competitions he would tell me to go out and deliver and say to me, 'Have balls.' I am always in a panic before competitions and London 2012 was no exception. Before the Olympic Games he said, 'Have you got your shin pads?' I checked. 'Have you got your belt?' Check. 'Have you got your helmet?' Check. 'Have you got your balls?' I didn't hear properly and panicked and started looking everywhere … until I realised! I laughed and knew I was courageous because of him. I could hear his words in my head: 'You're only a somebody when you get the medals.'

He is a real legend in the sport and that gave me confidence. I knew that if I could catch Paul, then I could catch any of my opponents. It had been my great ambition to hit him in the head and I managed it a few times ... but he hit me so many more! I will never be able to thank him for all his preparation and planning for me. He has a wife and family, yet he dedicated himself to giving me the best possible chance of success. He was committed to not leaving me at all. He would do extra sessions at seven o'clock in the morning, anything to give me the edge on my opponents. He wanted the win for me as much as I did. All his decisions for me are based on good intentions and when he needs to put me back on track I know that it's for the right reasons. He values the right codes of behaviour. I still phone his father, Brian, before each of my competitions. He is a wise man too, and I value them both and all that they have done for me.

The day before the competition Mum, Dad, Darren, Luke, Uncle Gary, Nana and Granddad all got a pass to come to meet me in GB House. We were allowed to be together for an hour. We were surrounded by all of the other athletes and their families, and it was like a dream to be around the very best athletes of Team GB. My mum was excited to be there, but very nervous for me. She kept looking at me as if to say 'Are you OK?', and was clearly worried about me. I gave her a look that immediately settled her. She knew I was equipped to do this. She took me aside and said to me, 'I couldn't be prouder than I am of you already.'

Granddad said just one thing as he left: 'Are you going to win it for me?' He says I replied, 'Yes, of course I am.' He could see it in my eyes. He was convinced, as he knows me inside out, and going back on the train he announced to the family, 'She's going to win tomorrow. I know it!' My mum had said the same earlier, too. She was crying and I had to reassure her and tell her not to worry about me. I had to show her I was strong and that I was determined to do this for her.

The night before the competition came so fast I couldn't believe that it was already here. The build-up had gone on and on but suddenly there was no turning back. Paul had helped me get here but now it was up to me.

Chapter Six

The BBC commentator at the time said it all: 'You little beauty!' Jade, just like Nicole Cooke before her, will have inspired a whole generation of young women to pursue their dreams. In two of the toughest Olympic sports they showed what desire, determination and focus can achieve in your chosen field.

Lynn Davies CBE, Olympic gold medallist
and President of UK Athletics

ExCeL, the international exhibition and convention centre, hosted Taekwondo for London 2012. It was a huge building and the first time I went there, the day before our event, the arena was empty and still. It looked amazing even with no lights to show off the space. All I could think of was that I had made it to the home Olympic Games. I just wanted to take it all in and enjoy the moment.

However, I was completely overwhelmed by how it had changed when I arrived for my first competition the next day. Paul had set up a room for us with our own food and drink and music and our very own taekwondo ring fitted with brand new mats to warm up on. He knew that I might get worried beforehand and he wanted to make sure that I was warmed up and ready. His plan was to make sure that I was in a strong physical and mental state to go out into the arena. He sparred with me and was deliberately intense, to switch me on to the occasion, and I was taken aback and had to sharpen up.

I suddenly understood why the Olympic Games is the biggest international sporting event. All around the arena were packed tiers of people, all waiting for the bouts to begin. The noise was deafening as the audience stamped and cheered along with the presenter. He was encouraging them to start a Mexican wave and to call out the names of the countries they were supporting. The shouts for Great Britain were by far the loudest. The chanting got louder and louder and Paul turned to me and said firmly, 'Don't look up. Wait until you get into the ring. Concentrate on what you're doing.' It was good advice. The more I saw and heard, the more nervous I got. I kept trying to take it all in and to use the atmosphere to help me focus on my task ahead. The crowd was with me and it seemed like Great Britain flags filled the room. But I couldn't help but look up as I heard people screaming my name over and over. It really made me jump! In the end it was the crowd that got me through, though, because they gave me the extra edge. Each time I went out, the screaming began and it lifted me. I normally have to look at the scoreboard to see if I have scored, but this time I didn't have to, the crowd's roar told me! I won the first match and we came back and started the warm-up all over again.

I did what Paul told me and concentrated on taking one fight at a time. He told me not to get ahead of myself and to concentrate on the job in hand, as one loss meant I would be out. He warned me not to get too confident and his words got me back on track, following his tactics to the letter as I had been taught. Without that lesson from Paul, I might have been complacent – my opponents were dangerous and wanted to win too! I had a rest before the semi-final as Paul advised, and we sat drinking tea and eating biscuits to relax.

When I got to the semi-final, it hit me that if I won I was guaranteed a medal. The girl I was fighting, Tseng Li-Cheng from Chinese Taipei, was ranked number one in the world and I had never fought her before. It was a hard fight and at the beginning I was down 2–0. In the third round, I thought: Right … I just have to go for it! I gave it everything I had, put pressure on her and went 3–2 up. She panicked and started to rush and I began to go ahead, getting a head shot and picking her off bit by bit. In the last seconds there were kicks going everywhere and it was so close. But then the bell went and I had won! The crowd erupted and the noise was deafening – a silver medal at least for Team GB!

The final was against the girl I had lost to in the World Championships, Hou Yuzhuo from China. She was the double World Champion. I wasn't thinking about that, as I was bouncing around knowing I had a silver medal, whatever happened. This probably really helped – I was so relaxed and happy I didn't have time to get nervous! Paul had to bring me down to earth and warned me, 'You still have one more fight. If you go home with a silver medal you'll be devastated.' As always, he was right and it was what I needed to hear. The gold medal was attainable.

I had banged my foot in the very first fight

and it began to get gradually more painful till I couldn't walk on it. I couldn't let any of my competitors see I had an injury or they would exploit the weakness. I had to pass the girl from China who I would be fighting, and I had to try to walk normally so she would have no idea I was hurting. I sent a text telling my family I couldn't walk and my mum was in tears for me saying, 'Don't go in. Don't fight!' As if I could even think of that – these were the Olympic Games, my ultimate dream! I had treatment on my foot just to be able to get to the arena. Paul talked through our tactics and we talked about how badly I wanted that gold medal. He reminded me, 'She took the World Championship from you – she won't take the Olympics!' I had to stick to our agreed tactics and not deviate to try to impress the crowd. Our preparation had been meticulous and I knew that I had to stick to the game plan to beat her.

As I made my way to the ring, the crowd noise swelled yet again. I couldn't believe it was possible for it to get any louder but it was. I remember saying to myself, 'She won't beat me again. I won't stop until I beat her.' I had to live up to my nickname 'The Headhunter' which was given to me by my fellow players at the

Academy because I always kick to the head – it gains more points. I drew myself up and got ready for the final fight. I couldn't bear to think about all those people special to me in the crowd who were willing me to win. They have no idea just how much they helped me that day. Their wall of support was amazing and made me dig in to find more to win. It was as if the arena was mine.

The people of Flint were watching at home. They were crowded into one pub and being filmed by the BBC. They ran out of beer that day and had to stock up in the local off licence as they had started at 10 a.m., despite knowing I wasn't coming on until the evening! My family, my former headteacher Mrs McClean and her husband (who had bought their tickets long before I had been selected), Brian's wife and Paul's little daughter, Abigail, were all at the ExCeL arena. My first coach, Martin Williams, had also come, together with many of my friends. My boyfriend Jordan was in the crowd too and I thought about his message the night before: 'You're better than anyone, so just believe it!' He knew how much this day meant, being an athlete himself. He was a huge support to me and understood the build-up to the competition as we were both focused on the same goals.

There were GB flags around the arena, plus the Welsh dragon flying high. It had to be my time. The announcer called out, 'Now here's the one you've all been waiting for ...'

The fight started and we were both cagey at first; the occasion had got to both of us. I remembered Paul saying quietly, 'You're the best,' and I remembered Granddad looking at me and mouthing, 'You're the best.' What helped me win was Paul saying to me at the beginning of the day, 'Go after your goal. Don't wait around for it.' Thinking of this switched me into the frame of mind I needed. I beat Hou Yuzhuo 6–4 to take the title. It was over – I had won! It was Great Britain's first ever taekwondo gold medal! I threw my hat up in the air and ran to Paul. People could see what I had just done, but he had put in as much effort as me and this win was for both of us. Ours is not just a player and coach relationship because we have known one another for so long. He is my hero and he is also a good friend. I jumped on him and tried to lift his hand up with mine to highlight that we were in this together. I wanted him to share the moment. I searched everywhere to see my family and jumped over to pick up flags to carry around the arena. The Welsh flag I picked up was from Mrs McClean, who, with her husband, had watched my victory from the front row. He threw two flags down to me, so draped with one Welsh flag and one GB flag, I ran around the arena, ecstatic with joy. We had done it! The crowd was absolutely awesome, screaming out my name and chanting, 'GB, GB, GB!' and I looked up at the video screens trying to take in all that was happening.

At the medal ceremony I was in a daze and I still couldn't find my family. As the moment arrived I was totally overwhelmed and couldn't decide what to do. The French fighter, who had won the bronze medal, was a big rival but I remember her being lovely to me and helping me out. 'This is for you,' she said. 'These are your people, so wave to them and celebrate with them. Enjoy your success.' The flags went up, the sound of the national anthem boomed around the room and people were cheering, waving and stamping their feet again. I sang my heart out, not wanting the moment to stop. Up in the stands, people were dancing and I couldn't believe what I was seeing. I threw my flowers into the crowd to thank them for their support.

Paul was ecstatic and the team jumped on me, congratulating me. Two of my teammates, Sarah Stevenson and Lutalo Muhammad, still had to compete and so had gone to bed early, but Lutalo told me later that he was so eager to know how I was doing that he was sneakily watching on his laptop not to miss anything. He said he blamed me for keeping him up. He was buzzing with my success and couldn't sleep despite having his own fight the next day! However, I couldn't have put him off too much as he won the bronze medal!

Back at the arena, all I wanted to do was to see my family, but I was bombarded by the media who all wanted interviews and kept telling me that I had made history. I was immediately asked to go with the drug-testing team as expected but I kept saying, 'Please, I have to see my family first.' They did allow me to do this but accompanied me as I rushed across to meet everyone. My mum was sobbing and gave me a big hug and told people that she couldn't believe that her little girl's dream had come true. Someone even took a photo of my mum saying that they had never seen anyone look so happy and wanted to capture that joy! I have a special bond with my mum. I was born on Mother's Day and she always says I am the best present she could ever have had. She is always smiling and positive and I was thrilled to see how happy I had made her that day.

I kept looking at my medal. I couldn't let it go. I had dreamt about the medal and I wasn't about to let it out of my sight. I got back to the Olympic Village finally at two o'clock in the morning and went to McDonald's with the team and ate everything I could. I had been healthy for so long and this was my opportunity to be naughty and eat what I wanted! I couldn't sleep for all the texts and messages from friends and unknown people across the world saying how pleased they were for me. I couldn't believe that I was getting all this attention. I got up to check the Internet to see what had been written about me. I kept thinking, did it really happen? It just didn't feel real. Twitter and Facebook were going wild and I kept reading message after message. My twitter followers went from a few to over forty thousand virtually overnight!

The closing ceremony was amazing. I could finally really enjoy my success and relax and take everything in. I was with the team – Sarah, Lutalo, Martin, the coaches and me – all enjoying the night. Team GB was the last team out and when we emerged the roar filled the stadium. The sound of clapping, cheering, whistling and stamping was phenomenal. Finally, we could all relax and we mingled with the other teams, congratulating each other and singing along to the bands. I loved seeing the Spice Girls – Girl Power! Lord Coe's speech reminded us, and the world, of why we had all taken part. The athletes had a big party afterwards. There were food stands, barbecues and great music, and everyone had a great time. I'd had no sleep for days, though, and finally it caught up with me. I would have loved to have stayed on but I was exhausted and had to go to bed! It was astonishing to think millions of people worldwide had been watching us, and that London 2012 was now officially over.

Chapter Seven

Jade has left a strong legacy in our school and community and she continues to inspire others. She has resilience, a positive attitude and a fighting spirit that we can all emulate no matter what our talent is. The school motto is 'Believe, Achieve, Succeed'. Jade does.

Mrs McClean, headteacher,
Flint High School

I took time off after the Olympic Games to go on a well-deserved holiday to Ibiza with my family and Jordan. He brought me back to earth when we did some training together on the hotel roof. We were play-sparring and, as usual, he didn't give any quarter and it turned into a real competition. He didn't give me any more respect than before the gold medal, trying to make sure he got the better of me! In the end we had to stop it as we were getting funny looks from passing holidaymakers.

It was lovely to relax and keep reminding myself that London 2012 really had happened.

I returned home to hundreds of congratulations cards, messages and gifts. I was even sent a gold toaster and kettle and a gold suitcase to celebrate my win! But the celebrations didn't stop there. Once back in Flint, there was an open-top-bus parade through the town, ending with a civic reception hosted by the Mayor. She had organised a party and a wonderful cake and I held the gold medal up proudly for the people of Flint who had been so good to me. She had asked that people put flags out and come to the town hall to support me. She needn't have worried. Hundreds of people turned out from start to finish and the fireworks were the perfect end to a fantastic day.

To mark my gold medal win, the Royal Mail painted a post box gold on Church Street in Flint. It's remarkable to think that it will stay that way, like many others across Britain, as a tribute to our performances. I went to see it for myself and began signing autographs in the light and finished in the dark. Every time I pass the post box I see people still having their photo taken next to it. I was also honoured with the twenty-fifth gold medal stamp awarded by the Royal Mail. The late evening time of my win meant that the stamp was the fastest the Royal Mail have ever produced. The team there had one hour to choose the image and add my name!

I was also proud to be part of the Welsh Olympians and Paralympians parade at the Senedd in Cardiff. Once again, hundreds of people turned out to see us all and we gathered on the steps of the Senedd building looking down at a sea of flags and waving arms, and hearing all the cheering. I stood alongside Tom James, Mark Colbourne and Aled Davies, marvelling at how many people kept arriving. The Welsh athletes had done well at the Olympic and Paralympic Games and I was proud to be one of them. First Minister Carwyn Jones spoke and then each of our names was read out for the crowd to cheer loudly while we, in turn, acknowledged their enthusiastic applause. I was overwhelmed again that people came out for us, even though the Games were over. A band played, a choir sang and we all agreed that it was a perfect ceremony. It ended with the anthems being sung loudly and ticker tape thrown. It couldn't get better than this. What a welcome home!

The next day I'd been invited to Old Trafford to show my gold medal to the crowd and was presented with a special Manchester United shirt emblazoned with 'Jones 2012'. I got to meet some of the players before the game. It was a great afternoon for my granddad, my brother and me. It was good for Manchester United too as they beat Wigan Athletic 4–0. It was the first time I had seen Manchester United live, and walking on to the pitch as my team were warming up and hearing the fans cheer for me was unbelievable. I'm a passionate Manchester United fan and had to keep telling myself this was really happening.

A short time later, I made a very emotional return journey to Flint High School, which will always be an important part of my life. My mum and my auntie were former pupils and my brother is there now. On the day in question, I walked into the school assembly, not to the morning hymn, but to the pounding beat of 'The Eye of the Tiger'. I felt ten feet tall – teachers and pupils were crying and giving me a rapturous welcome. Seeing my little brother listening to my assembly was surreal. I could remember sitting where he was and listening to a special visitor who had come in to speak. The whole school was present. I wore my GB kit with my gold medal around my neck. It was my way of saying thank you to the people and the place where it all had started. Appropriately, they had even put on a taekwondo demonstration by my first coach's club. I am very proud of my school and I hope the school staff and pupils are proud of me, too.

In November 2012, I was delighted to be the guest of honour at the renaming of Flint Pavilion as the Jade Jones Pavilion in recognition of my Olympic win. I was thrilled that they thought so much of my achievement and particularly pleased that a leisure centre, which would encourage more participation in sport, would have my name. I still go there sometimes to do sessions when I am home. I am so proud of being from Flint and when I was later asked to turn on the Christmas lights, it was the perfect end to the year.

I was also invited to be a guest at the Pride of Britain awards. This is an award ceremony to honour Britain's unsung heroes and I was nervous but joined with Nicola Adams, Britain's first female Olympic boxing champion, and Tom Daley, the bronze medallist diver. We sat, watching people like Simon Cowell and Amanda Holden arrive, thinking it was amazing that we were there. However, the real stars were those who won the awards and I was completely in awe hearing their stories. Their tales were outstanding and their medals truly hard won. We were able to meet all of the award-winners later and spent time congratulating them on their phenomenal achievements.

I also joined Matt Dawson's team for BBC's *A Question of Sport 2012 Olympics Special*. I was with the canoe slalom champions Tim Baillie and Etienne Stott. On Phil Tufnell's team were the double gold-medal-winning cyclist Laura Trott and the long jump gold medallist Greg Rutherford. Matt Dawson and Phil Tufnell were great with the audience, laughing and joking and everyone was having a good time. It came to my question and I was asked for the name of the Japanese fighter I had gone up against in the quarter final. I had no idea. Matt grinned saying, 'You must know, Jade.' I tried to guess and everyone was laughing. It was no good, I didn't know. My coach had always said that when you go out to fight you are fighting the country, not the girl. I therefore always knew her as Japan. That's how I had been taught to think and prepare for a fight.

I was named as BBC Wales Sports Personality of the Year at the Millennium Stadium in Cardiff, ahead of rugby player Dan Lydiate in second place and cyclist Geraint Thomas in third place. I couldn't believe, looking at the list of great Welsh contenders, that it was possible. It was a magical night winning the public vote and I was thrilled. I saw it as a vote for my sport. Once again though, my timing for an awards ceremony went wrong and I ended up having to change into my outfit in a Tesco store on the way because I was running so late! I was also given *The Sunday Times* Young Olympian of the Year award, the UK Sport award for the outstanding figure, twenty-one years of age or younger, at the London 2012 Olympic Games.

At Christmas, there was a BBC *Superstars 2012* Olympic Special. Sixteen of us GB teammates – eight men and eight women – competed against each other to be crowned the two best all-round superstars. We had to compete in eight different disciplines: 100 metres and 800 metres, on the track, the javelin, the pool, kayaking, cycling, archery and then gym tests. Everyone talked about the great Superstars competitions of the past and that made me more nervous than ever. We had all taken time off after the Olympic Games but a competitive edge came out in all of us. Once on the line none of us would give anything less than one hundred per cent and it made us all laugh to see how we reacted. We **all** wanted to win! Denise Lewis and Iwan Thomas were the presenters and they were having a great time. I was the youngest competitor but gave it all I had. I surprised myself in the running and I was proud of my dips in the gym test, but in the swimming competition I was awful and up against some really good swimmers. My performance was not helped by the fact I hated the swimming cap, which was the most unattractive thing ever! The boxer, Anthony Joshua, and the oarswoman, Helen Glover, were the eventual winners, to cheers from the rest of us. The weather was dreadful but we all kept smiling to the end.

The ultimate honour was to receive an MBE in the New Year's Honours list. I joined other Olympic and Paralympic athletes at Buckingham Palace to meet Prince Charles and collect my award. Katherine Copeland, the women's rowing lightweight double sculls gold medallist, and I proudly held up our medals and stood with Ellie Simmonds and Dame Sarah Storey, amazed that we had been given these honours. To have Prince Charles wish me good luck for my future is something I could never have imagined happening to me.

Chapter Eight

Jade's not famous for being a reality star. She IS the real deal. She's a strong woman and wins by sheer hard work. Everything she achieves is down to her own determination and hard graft.

Jamie Baulch, three-times World
Champion 400 metres

People ask me what the best and worst things are about being an elite athlete. I always say that the worst thing is getting up in the mornings for training – I'm hopeless at getting out of bed! The best thing is easy … I love being with the team. There is nothing better because it's what I have always wanted to do. I think I am really fortunate to be doing something that I love. The coaching staff and the performance director work hard on our schedules and it's up to us to give our best. We all have good and bad days but it's how you react to those days that matters. I'm always nervous before a fight. Nobody wants to lose, so I listen to my coach and up my game accordingly. I put my favourite track on, crank my headphones up and listen to the words of Eminem's 'Lose Yourself'. The opening always sets me up: 'Look, if you had one shot, or one opportunity to seize everything you ever wanted, one moment, would you capture it or just let it slip?' It works for me.

My work with the Jaguar Academy of Sport is important, as it is a chance for me to give something back. It is a privilege to go to the Jaguar days and be able to talk to up-and-coming athletes and share my thoughts and ideas on how to be the best you can be. As an ambassador, I can honestly show that hard work pays off and dreams can come true. One of my dreams came true when I was invited to the Jaguar plant in Castle Bromwich, Birmingham, to visit the production line to talk about my Olympic experience and see my own Jaguar car being made! I was collected in a chauffeur-driven Jaguar and felt like royalty as I arrived. I'm used to getting the train, not being personally chauffered! I was with Jamie Baulch, another great British athlete and ambassador, and it was an exciting moment to walk into the company and see over a hundred people who all stood clapping and cheering me. Geoff

Cousins from the Academy showed us around the production line and everywhere we looked there were spectacular cars. Everyone at the plant was proud of their efforts to present me with my car. I had never had such special treatment. I couldn't believe that I'd be driving around in my own Jaguar car – a British-made award-winning car given to a British champion! I had to undergo a training course and at first I was petrified because it was such a big car. I'd gone from a Mini to this! Also, I'd never driven an automatic car before. We went straight out on to the motorway and I was told, 'Put your foot down.' I was scared but it was to teach me to have confidence in my ability and the car's. I worried that if I made any mistakes they might take the car back!

I'm setting my goals for the future. I'm not World Champion yet or European Champion. I want to go to Rio for the next Olympic Games. I want to be the best I can possibly be. I have had a great deal of support from my family and friends and the very best coaches. They have all gone way beyond the call of duty for me and I am privileged to have had this. It is important that I conduct myself well and win well in the future. I want to give back to other young sportsmen and women the help that has been extended to me. I take my mentoring role seriously and look forward to sharing my experiences and knowledge with others. I enjoy presenting taekwondo training seminars because I want to promote the sport. I hope more people will take it up and understand the real benefits it brings.

For me, training hard for hours a day is tough but when it pays off and you become a champion it is all worthwhile. I want to make my family proud. Taekwondo has given me a sport I love, great friends, and the chance to travel and see places I would never have seen otherwise. I have met extraordinary people who I would never otherwise have met and I am still surprised and excited by what has happened. Outside of sport, my life is about socialising with my friends and Jordan, listening to music and relaxing ... and of course, shopping!

Nothing worth anything comes easily and I have to keep working hard but I am prepared for that and look forward to the challenges ahead.

Quick Reads 📖

Books in the Quick Reads series

Quick Reads 📖

Fall in love with reading

Do not go Gentle
Phil Carradice
*A story based on the life and death of poet
Dylan Thomas*

Accent Press

November 1953, and Dylan Thomas, Britain's finest poet, is dying in a hospital bed in New York. What brought him to this end is not clear. But he is a man tormented by fear – fear of failing as a writer, fear of a marriage doomed to end in disaster, even fear of death itself – all of which have led him to find comfort in alcohol, outrageous behaviour, and the arms of other women.

Now, as Dylan lies waiting for the end, he thinks back over his life, from his childhood in Swansea to his days as a wild young poet in London, from his tempestuous marriage to Caitlin MacNamara to his final weeks in New York.

Dylan Thomas may not have wanted to die but he had little desire to live. *Do Not Go Gentle* paints a picture of a man who has clearly reached the end of his tether.

Quick Reads 📖

Fall in love with reading

Lionheart
Richard Hibbard

Accent Press

When Lions and Wales rugby star Richard Hibbard crashed into George Smith under a clear night sky in Australia, it felt as though the tremors might have rocked Sydney Harbour Bridge.

Smith was the 'Mr Indestructible' of Australian rugby, yet he was helped off the pitch. Hooker Hibbard simply shook his trademark blond locks and carried on helping the Lions earn their 2013 series victory. Soon, pictures of "Hibbz" celebrating in the dressing room with James Bond actor Daniel Craig were being beamed around the world.

In *Lionheart*, the Ospreys star reflects on his long and often rocky road to the top of world rugby: from his roots in Port Talbot, to his stint with rugby league club Aberavon Fighting Irish, to himself fighting back from countless serious injuries.

About the Author

Born in north Wales in 1993, Jade Jones became the first Briton to win a gold medal for taekwondo, in the London 2012 Olympic Games. She went on to win the public vote for the BBC Wales Sports Personality of the Year 2012 and was appointed Member of the Order of the British Empire (MBE) in the 2013 New Year Honours, for services to taekwondo.